The Bride's Blemish!

Dr. Heather Owen

(first in the Joy series)

Published by

Precious Oil
PUBLICATIONS
www.preciousoil.com/publications

ISBN 13: 978-1-7384365-2-1

ISBN 10:   1-7384365-2-7

First published **2024**

Precious Oil PUBLICATIONS
www.preciousoil.com/publications

10a Listooder Road, Crossgar, Downpatrick, Northern Ireland BT30 9JE

Contents

Prologue

by Rev. Dr. Mark Rivera, CET* Theotherapy,
Christian Counselling International (2021)

The Bride's Blemish is a book that demonstrates the courage to write on difficult subjects and the desire to expand on a Theotherapeutic topic, offering clarity to assist those seeking answers. It helps give direction and find biblical answers to some of life's conundrums.

In the depths of human existence lies a yearning for understanding, a thirst for clarity amidst life's myriad complexities. Humans are creatures driven by an insatiable desire to make sense of the world around them, to find answers that bring solace to their troubled hearts. Yet, there are subjects we deem difficult, areas of inquiry we shy away from, fearing the weight they might bear upon our souls.

It is within this realm of difficult subjects that I invite you, dear reader, to embark on a journey of exploration. In *The Bride's Blemish*, Dr. Heather Owen dares traverse the uncharted territories of human experience, addressing the courage required to write on these sensitive topics and the profound desire to expand our understanding of the Theotherapeutic subjects that lie beyond our comfort zones.

But what is meant by *'Theotherapeutic'?* It is a term coined from the modality of Christian counselling called *Theotherapy*, used to describe those subjects that touch upon the wounds and blemishes of the human soul, the areas of struggle and vulnerability that we often keep hidden from the world. These are the subjects that challenge our preconceptions, push us to confront our biases, and demand that we extend compassion

---

* Chief Executive Theotherapist

to ourselves and others, by learning to forgive and love those that hurt us.

Why, you may ask, should we venture into such difficult terrain? The answer, my dear reader, lies in our collective longing for growth, healing, and spiritual maturation. It is in the face of adversity and uncertainty that we are offered the greatest opportunities for transformation. By facing the blemishes of our lives head-on, we invite divine grace to work within us, bringing about a restoration that surpasses our wildest dreams.

Within these pages, Dr. Owen draws upon the wisdom of Holy Scripture, the teachings of faith, and the insights of psychology to shed light on these Theotherapeutic subjects. She delves into the depths of human brokenness, exploring topics such as trauma, addiction, grief, and mental health, among others. Together, she seeks to discern the timeless truths embedded within the Bible, unearthing answers that offer hope, direction, and guidance in the face of life's most perplexing conundrums.

I invite you to approach this journey with an open heart and a willingness to embrace discomfort. Let us not shy away from the difficult, but instead, let us lean into it, trusting that through the power of God's precious divine love, we will find the strength to confront our own blemishes and extend compassion to the blemished hearts of others.

May this book serve as a beacon of light, illuminating the path towards wholeness and authenticity. May it also embolden you to write on difficult subjects, to engage in rigorous exploration, and to seek the face of God amidst life's complexities. And may it remind you that, in the end, it is through courage, compassion, and the transformative power of God's loving grace that we find our truest selves and bring healing to a broken world.

Rev. Dr. Mark Rivera CET*-CCI,

San Juan, Puerto Rico

---

* Chief Executive Theotherapist

Introduction

This short book is for believers in the church who wish to pursue deeper, loving relationships that are truly satisfying and fulfilling. Strong platonic relationships with the opposite sex will encourage the foundation for future strong marital relationships, which will allow individuals to reflect God's design for marriage.

This platform of strong relationships is not just for married couples but for singles too. However, the focus is on how marriage reflects the picture of Christ and His Bride and of that deep, longing hope for the coming Christ. The Bridegroom, who is Jesus Christ, will return for His Church, the Bride of Christ. So, this book will explore how to develop relationships that will be beneficial and helpful for all individuals in life.

The gospel of Jesus Christ states that, *'Christ came into the world'* (**John 18:37**), *'took on our humanity'* (**John 1:14**), *'lived without sin'* (**Hebrews 4:13-15**), *'died in our place for our sins'* (**Romans 5:8**), that *'He was buried and three days later rose again'* (**1 Corinthians 15:3-4**), and *'will return for all who believe in Him'* (**Matthew 24:30-31**). In the meantime, before His return for all who believe in Him, there is a time of waiting until He appears.

This time of waiting can produce mixed feelings in believers because we live in the *'here and now'* with *'the future immediacy'* of Christ's return. This struggle is a dialectical tension (that is, two ideas in parallel to each other that create tension) proposed originally by Socrates c. 470–399 BC and Plato c. 424–347 BCE; and this struggle is real as we continue to live out our everyday lives, knowing that there is a better life in the future.

The believers who have gone before us experienced this same dilemma of the *'waiting'* period. The Thessalonians (**2**

Thessalonians 3:6ff) had to be corrected in their response to this issue, as some considered it right to stop making future plans and stopped working. This response was obviously not good, so we need to learn the right approach of *'waiting'* for Christ's return. Hopefully, we can learn from those who have gone before.

Heroes of the faith waited for the promise of their visions to be fulfilled, yet some died *'in faith'* not having received the promises given to them by God. **Hebrews 11:13-16**

Their faith in these unfulfilled promises kept them believing because it was not the promise per se, that was important, but the relationship they had with their heavenly Father. This relationship sustained them in holding onto the promise because it originated from a covenant keeping God.

Their relationship was not dependent on themselves but on a covenant basis and this will be explored. This covenantal relationship is important because if it is not grounded in Scripture and applied, it will not sustain us in the time *'we wait'* for Christ's return.

So, we need to address why it can be difficult to live in the *'here and now,'* while waiting for the fulfilment of the promise to one day be with Christ where He is. **Ephesians 2:6** He is coming again – will He find us ready, anticipating His return? **Malachi 3:2, 4:1** (Amplified bible)

1 – The Bride

- **God's directive**

- **False assumptions**

- **Preparations - Esther**

- **Removal of spot and wrinkle**

- **Syncretism**

- **People pleasing**

- **Transformation**

When we talk of the bridegroom and the bride, we have an understanding that this relationship is founded and grounded in love – an expression that is deep, personal and intimate. The outward expression of this love is usually given when the couple get engaged; however, in the current society's culture, another picture is presented, where the couple who say they love each other, choose to live together.

Some couples reason that marriage is an outdated institution and unnecessary, so the beginning of a relationship on this basis projects a trial-and-error approach, a quasi-state of a marriage relationship; which leaves the door open to end the relationship, if one or the other feels it's not working out as expected.

Couples live together as a way of trying out marriage to test compatibility with their partners, while still having the option of ending the relationship without legal implications – **Manning, Smock**, (2009).

There are 3.5 million cohabiting couples in England and Wales as of 2020, up 137% from 1.5 million in 1996 – **UK Parliament**. Common law marriage and cohabitation.pdf.

And 90% of couples lived together before a civil ceremony and 81% lived together before a religious ceremony. But only 22% of marriages have a religious ceremony – **Divorce Rate UK** [21+ Mind-Boggling Facts & Stats] (review42.com) ONS, Kabic, 2022).

The effect of every relationship has consequences and when the couple begin it by cohabiting, they become intertwined together – emotionally, financially, sexually – without any safeguards if the relationship breaks up. However, co-habitation laws have changed recently, to ensure that couples do not lose out financially as a result of the commitments they have put into this relationship.

Couples can even agree to sign a legal cohabitation agreement. In this contract both parties outline how they will divide their current assets and liabilities if they end their committed relationship with each other. This is because cohabiters do not have the same protection as those who are married, or who have agreed to a registered civil partnership. This sets up the relationship as a business contract, which means that either party can end the contract, if they do not see themselves benefiting from it.

Despite this, the emotional separation hurts just as deeply, as when a couple pursues the biblical, conventional and traditional legal route towards marriage. The trial-and-error approach leaves an escape route; and falters in the sense that it doesn't encourage a long-term attitude towards the relationship. The entanglement becomes more complicated if the relationship creates children out of marriage. However, many relationships do start off this way and appear to be successful as they continue to live together.

Some who begin this way may eventually go on and pursue marriage; others when they encounter issues break up and sometimes move on to other partners. This encourages serial relational monogamy – each new relational connection accumulating more emotional angst. The baggage, if not addressed, is then taken into the next relationship.

It is not uncommon for relationships to have engaged in second or third families – whether living together, civil partnerships or remarried. Households containing multiple families were the fastest growing type of household over the last two decades, having increased by ¾ to 297,000 households in 2019. (Census, 2021).

God's directive

The biblical directive is to act appropriately, honouring the individuals concerned by giving the commitment that is required in the way that God desired. **1 Corinthians 7:9**

So, to avoid the issue of fornication – that is sex before marriage – couples following God's directive will get engaged, then wait until after marriage for sexual expression.

However, engagement is not a requirement, but a declaration of intent that separates the couple from all other relationships, while they wait for the culmination of the wedding day, which will seal legally the exclusivity of the relationship for the forthcoming bridegroom and bride. It is a declaration of a covenant commitment based on love, faith and trust. It is a witness to their peers, family and before God that these two individuals have committed themselves to each other.

On this understanding, the couple prepare for spending their lives together. Pre-marital counselling is useful here, so that the couple is aware of how this commitment together will affect them (Wright, 1992). This is a time of preparing for change. To share your life with another 24/7 will always bring up issues that have not been envisaged when discussing this future prospect.

False assumptions

Some couples make the mistake that once the commitment has been made then what they do not like in the other, they can change, or try to change, to manipulate the relationship to be what was imagined beforehand. This rarely works and increases marital disharmony and conflicts. Couples need to be open minded and realistic about the demands and challenges of an intimate relationship.

Many couples rush headlong in without stopping to consider what and how to deal with conflicts that may arise. Preparation for these times may prevent so many relationships from breaking up. *Relate* – a relational counselling service – state that if couples in conflict came in for counselling earlier many relationships could be saved from breaking up.

In the UK, in 2021, 42% of marriages in England and Wales ended in divorce. However, the divorce rate has been falling since the 1980's, possibly due to the fact that less couples are marrying and more living together than before (*Crisp & Co.*). It was found that more women initiate divorce (62%) than men (*ONS*).

The average length of time for marriage before divorce is now 12.3 years (*ONS*). During the previous pandemic lockdown there was an increase of 95% in divorce enquiries (*Independent*). Unreasonable behaviour (46%) is cited as the most common cause of divorce; the second, after two-year separation with consent and the third is adultery (10.5%) (*NimbleFins*).

60% of all divorce petitions listed a fault-based grounds for divorce; of these 70% said it made the divorce process more bitter. 21% said it also made child maintenance more difficult to deal with. 31% said it also made the financial settlement more complicated (*BBC*).

Divorce day is known as the day for most divorces, which is the first working Monday after Christmas (*Evening Standard*). In 2021 the divorce rate increased 230% in the first week of January alone! The reason being financial difficulty after the holiday break, increasing stress on the relationship. 11% of divorcees are second ones for one partner (*Crisp & Co.*) and 30% of long marriages, over 30 years, end in divorce and the rate has climbed since 1993. (*NimbleFins*).

However, in the UK new divorce laws have come into effect from April, 2022. The *Divorce, Dissolution and Separation Act, 2020* makes it easier to reduce the potential for conflict amongst divorcing couples by removing the ability to make allegations about the conduct of a spouse, and it allows divorcees to apply to end their marriage jointly and focus on other important issues like the children, property and finances. The terms have also been revised from *'decree nisi'* and *'decree absolute'* to *'conditional order'* and *'final order'*.

This Act also allows for a 20-week cooling off period from the start of the application for divorce, until the conditional order. This is supposed to encourage a period of reflection concerning the oncoming event. Subsequently, the changes also mean that divorce proceedings cannot be contested once the conditional order has been agreed.

These false assumptions need to be exposed and challenged before the marriage is engaged in – therefore, it is necessary to be as prepared as possible for the future event. To challenge any assumptions we will look at what the Scripture teaches us.

Preparation

So, time is taken for the bride's preparation. We read of Esther's example, where she was taken into King Xerxes' harem. **Esther 2**

Here all the chosen young maidens were set aside for a year, to be prepared to have an audience with the king. In this time, Esther, along with the other maidens, was given the best of things for purification with oils and spices, food, maids, accommodation, etc., to present themselves in all their glory as it were. So, Esther was shown favour by the King and was made Queen, in place of Vashti.

9

Esther was selected because she was already beautiful to behold. Her God-given gift of beauty was enhanced by the care she was given in the harem. God used Esther's gift to serve Him, for such a time as this, to fulfil God's purposes to the Jews. **Esther 4:14**

Esther was beautiful, yet she was still a sinner. In the same way, the church too is beautiful because it represents God – however, it is full of sinners who are saved by grace; so, as the *'Bride'* she needs to be prepared for the Bridegroom for His return.

We read that, *'Christ loved the church and gave Himself up for her, that He might sanctify and cleanse her with the washing of water by the Word, that He might present her to Himself a glorious church, not having spot or wrinkle or any such thing, but that she should be holy and without blemish.'* **Ephesians 5:25-27**

It goes on to speak of nourishing, protecting and cherishing the wife, as Christ does the church. *'This is a mystery, speaking of the relationship of the husband and wife, as Christ and the church.'* **Ephesians 5:32ff**

The time of *'waiting'* for the Bridegroom's coming is the time of preparation for the church – the body of Christ. The church prepared in all its glory is beautiful to behold. *'The new holy city, the new Jerusalem, descending out of heaven, from God, all arrayed like a bride beautified and adorned for her husband.'* **Revelation 21:2**

'Come with me! I will show you the Bride, the Lamb's wife ... clothed in God's glory, the lustre of it resembled a rare and most precious jewel, like jasper, shining clear as crystal.' **Revelation 21:9-11**

Perfect in every way, reflecting God in all his light, *'illuminating everything, as the Lamb is the light of the world.'* **Revelation 21:23**

'Blessed are those who have cleansed their garments, so they can approach the tree of life and enter the gates of the city.' **Revelation 22:14**

Removing every spot and wrinkle

So, the preparation is getting rid of everything – every spot and wrinkle, every sin that is opposed to God. In Revelation, we have lists of characteristics that will prevent individuals from entering into the marriage supper of the Lamb. In **Revelation 21:8** (amp) we read: *'But as for the cowards and unbelieving and abominable [who are devoid of character and personal integrity and practice or tolerate immorality], and murderers, and sorcerers [with intoxicating drugs], and idolaters and occultists [who practice and teach false religions], and all the liars [who knowingly deceive and twist truth], their part will be in the lake that blazes with fire and brimstone, which is the second death.'*

And **Revelation 21:7** (amp): *'and nothing that defiles or profanes or is unwashed will ever enter it, nor anyone who practices abominations [detestable, morally repugnant things] and lying, but only those [will be admitted] whose names have been written in the Lamb's Book of Life'.*

Revelation 22:3 (amp): *'There will no longer exist any-thing that is cursed [because sin and illness and death are gone]; and the throne of God and of the Lamb will be in it, and His bond-servants will serve and worship Him [with great awe and joy and loving devotion)'.*

Revelation 22:15 (amp): *'Outside are the dogs [the god-less, the impure, those of low moral character] and the sorcerers [with their intoxicating drugs, and magic arts], and the immoral persons [the perverted, the molesters, and the adulterers], and the murderers, and the idolaters, and everyone who loves and practices lying (deception, cheating)'.*

This list above needs to be read again so that we do not get confused, *'Woe to those who call evil good and good evil, who*

*put darkness for light and light for darkness, who put bitter
for sweet and sweet for bitter!'* **Isaiah 5:20**

Our confusion has been exacerbated by the lack of good
teaching and sound doctrine in the church today, resulting in
easily justifying and excusing our thoughts, emotions, behaviours,
attitudes, etc. Good teaching based on God's Word will challenge
us; *'it is living and powerful and sharper than any two-edged
sword, piercing even to the soul and spirit, and of joints and
marrow, and is a discerner of the thoughts and intents of the
heart.'* **Hebrews 4:12**

Today, teaching can be man-centred and feeling-orientated,
giving a feel-good factor which is popular. This sensationalist
approach encourages positive feelings, giving instant gratification
and quick fix answers. There is no negativity nor struggles here,
leading to an unrealistic view of life. Everything is great, good,
exciting etc. but sets people up for disappointments, as their
theology encounters, and clashes with, real life events.

Disappointments bring disillusionments and doubts that
God is who He's proclaimed to be – doubts of His love, when
life's trials begin. This popularist teaching doesn't equip people
to deal with the sufferings that will inevitably come in life,
which may turn them away from God. It sets them up for
failure, believing that God has failed them – because He
didn't produce the healings, the miracles, the outcomes, etc.,
that were prayed for and claimed in faith.

This teaching attracts those who want the gifts, but not the
'Giver'. The gifts can be anything secular or spiritual that will
enable us to reach our self-actualised goals, to achieve what
we want. God is good all the time when He answers our
prayers in the way we think He should – this view is not the
God of the Bible!

God is interested in our character to make us more Christ-
like, not for our convenience or comfort. Even Christ *'learned
obedience through the things that He suffered.'* **Hebrews 5:8**

Our goal must be Christ-centred not self-centredness: *'For
the time will come when people will not put up with sound*

*doctrine. Instead, to suit their own desires, they will gather around them a great number of teachers to say what their **itching ears** want to hear.'* **2 Timothy 4:3** (my bold type)

Impact of syncretism – compromise with the world

This popularist view has taken root over the years as more believers have moved away from God's Word by integrating the world's views on cultural issues alongside the Bible – in the name of being inclusive and seeker friendly, the modern church is guilty of syncretism.

But to align ourselves with the world's standards is to become an enemy of God.' **Rom. 12:2, James 4:4**

Yet we are specifically told in **Rev. 22:18-19** that, *'anyone who adds to these things, God will add to him the plagues that are written in this book, and if anyone takes away from the words of the book of this prophecy, God shall take away his part from the Book of Life, for the holy city and from the things which are written in this book'.* This is a warning that if we indulge in adapting the Word of God we will be called to account.

The decline of biblical teaching and an *exegetical* hermeneutic (an interpretation of scripture) approach that looks at the text in context and the original intent of the author; is leading people towards an *eisegesis* interpretation, that is reliant on how I feel about a particular passage and moves away from the context and meaning, to become a pretext.

This latter interpretation has to try and incorporate the current society's views and manipulates the Word to comply with a 21st century understanding. This is a syncretic view that compromises God's Word and weakens its power, making it impotent. As a consequence the Church imitates society, making it irrelevant to people's lives, and invalidating its voice and witness to that society. The Church needs to regain her boldness and confidence in God's Word and be God's mouthpiece to the world again in standing up for truth.

People pleasing

We love to gravitate to like-minded people because this makes us feel secure and comfortable. We do not like to be challenged on our understanding of God's Word. You hear the adage that, *'this is your understanding or interpretation'*, to justify their position. This encourages a relativistic view of the Word of God.

This view causes us to accommodate everyone and so we begin to alter and change what is not comfortable or convenient to us, or we think others want to hear. For example, if God is a God of love, then He loves and accepts everyone, therefore it's okay to indulge in sinful expressions – be an adulterer, live together, change your sexuality, practice homosexuality, be a paedophile, be a fraudster, liar, addict, etc. – because God loves you and if He loves you then He will forgive you?

However, God's forgiveness comes as a result of confession of our sin and repentance – which is a turning away from the sin and engaging in behaviours that God describes from His Word. **1 John 1:9**

God does forgive when there is repentance, but there is a price to be paid for the consequences of every sin. **Romans 6:23** The price is heavy because the outcome of sins are to steal, kill and destroy the individual. **John 10:10**

For example, the sin of lust that leads a married spouse to commit adultery may end with the marriage being lost and all the consequences this sin entails – family breakup, affecting the children, financial distress, increased stresses and anxieties, etc.

God does love us, but He is also a Holy God. His holiness means that God is also the Judge and will call us all to account for our compromising with the world. But the Perfect Judge looks beyond the presentation of our actions to our internal motives. Therefore, God – the Perfect Judge – looks on the heart, not on the outward manifestation of what we present as our Christian witness.

But the LORD said to Samuel, *'Do not look on his appearance or on the height of his stature, because I have rejected him. For the LORD sees not as man sees: man looks on the outward appearance, but the LORD looks on the heart.'* **1 Samuel 16:7**

Therefore, it's not about how we present ourselves to others, who may judge by our outward appearance, but what God sees – because we cannot fool God. The Pharisees were exemplary in their religious observances and traditions, but Christ claimed, *'they praise me with their lips but their hearts are far from me.'* **Isaiah 29:13, Matthew 15:8**

Transformation

So, the list from Revelation quoted above is not about a behavioural change, but addressing the internal motivations that move men and women to express such behaviours towards God, towards others and towards themselves. **1 Thessalonians 5:23**

It's important to address the issues internally first because changing the behaviours externally doesn't necessarily deal with the internal distress. Once the internal is healed the changes will manifest externally – this is the essence of transformation.

Focusing on the external behavioural change – for example, getting a child to behave externally by a mother's stern look – may not alter the rebellion that is felt internally by the child. Therefore, we need the transformative power of God to change us from within first. God wants to transform us into the likeness of His Son, not just change us to be acceptable to others. **Romans 12:1-2**

In this examination, we need the Holy Spirit's revelation to reveal us to ourselves, *'Search me, O God, and know my heart! Try me and know my anxieties! And see if there is any wicked way in me and lead me in the way everlasting.'* **Psalm 139:23-24**

Because *'the heart is deceitful above all things. And desperately wicked; who can know it? I the Lord know and search the heart; I test the mind ...'* **Jeremiah 17:9-10**

We deceive ourselves and therefore we need help and encouragement from godly men and women, whom God will use to help us come face to face with ourselves. This is not a comfortable or easy thing to do, but those who truly love God will humble themselves and face this process, no matter how painful it will be. **1 Peter 5:6-7**

But God gives courage to help and strengthen us. **1 Chronicles 28:20**

The courageous are the overcomers, as we overcome with Christ's help. Overcoming strengthens our faith, increasing our stability and security in our relationship with God. It increases our peace, our hope, our joy, our love, as we overcome the obstacles and difficulties we face.

This enables us to deal more ably with the sin we face, and the devil who battles for our very souls. As we overcome, our relationships become more enriched. Our sense of belonging increases. Our confidence in Christ grows, which enables us to encourage and help others who also encounter similar conflicts.

As we share the same comfort that God gives us and what it has taught us about ourselves and about God, then that knowledge can be shared to encourage others to mature and grow too. **2 Corinthians 1:4, Ephesians 4:12**

'And they overcame, conquered him by means of the blood of the Lamb and by the utterance of their testimony, for they did not love and cling to life even when faced with death, holding their lives cheap till they had to die for their witnessing.' **Revelation 12:11** (amp)

So, the next chapter will help us in dealing with the internal angst, so that we can implement the ability that God gives to us to be those overcomers in Christ.

2 Not behavioural modification

- Dealing with desires

- Relational conflicts

- Dealing with relational conflicts

- Right way to deal with relational conflicts

- Rejected people reject others

- Bridge of conflict resolution

- Tools of Theotherapy

- Dealing with the conflict that still needs God's healing

- Relational distress is seen in the Bride

- What is the right fear of God?

Dealing with desires

Consequently, if it's not about behavioural modification – that is, changing the external behaviours – and is an internal issue, we need to discover how or why our desires, thoughts, feelings and behaviours are leading us against God's will. In **James 1:14ff** (amp) we read, *'every person is tempted when he is drawn away, enticed and baited by his own evil desire, lust or passions. Then that evil desire, when it has conceived, gives birth to sin and sin when it is fully matured brings forth death.'*

So, it is our desires that we need to address. These desires come out of our needs and these are worked out in relationships. These are manifested in three basic relationships – with God, with others and towards the self.

Our desire to relate to God is worked out by deepening our love towards Him and receiving more of His love within, enjoying His presence, experiencing His Holy Spirit, through an intimate relationship that freely communicates with our Heavenly Father, increasing our awareness of who God is. This has to be fundamentally the most important relationship we have to keep us secure and sustain us throughout life.

To continue to be the better *'me'* that is increasingly more Christ centred, is to find fulfilment within ourselves, satisfying our desires and becoming all that God has created us to be. God's word states that, *'we are being changed from glory to glory.'* **1 Corinthians 3:18**

This is achieved by dealing with the internal sinful angst that we experience daily, that becomes cumulative throughout life, hindering the fulfilment of our potential. A better *'me'* frees us to enjoy an internal peace that is congruent within the self, integrated and whole, so there is an acceptance of who the self is. This develops and defines the self with a strong identity that manifests a strong self-worth and self-esteem, giving a secure and stable personality that has confidence in its own authority given by God.

Our desires are worked out with others for their fulfilment; others may help or hinder those desires, in using us, abusing us, or working with us to achieve those desires. We need others to fulfil our dreams, hopes and aspirations, etc. – whether that be for opportunities, finances, relational networking, or resources, etc. So our *'desires'* are worked out in relational connections – the saying that, *'it's not what you know, but who you know,'* is often true.

However, the angst comes when those relational connections go awry – the opportunities may not present themselves, or provision not be available, or others do not see your vision, e.g. as in Joseph's presentation of his dream to his brothers (**Genesis 37:5**), or others may be promoted, favoured, encouraged, etc., except you!

That hits home every time, yet we can rejoice in the fact that God who gives the desires, will fulfil them according to His time and purposes – just as he did for Joseph. Joseph had to go through a period where God was preparing him for the role that he would play in the future as the Prime Minister of Egypt.

In this time, Joseph had to learn to trust and depend on God, despite what his circumstances were saying to him. The fulfilment of Joseph's dreams, that motivated His desires, seemed hopeless that they would be fulfilled in his prison cell, so they had to die until God's perfect timing. In the same way, sometimes the things that we desire and want have to die, and we have to surrender and let them go, to wait God's perfect timing. *'I say to you, unless a grain of wheat falls into the ground and dies, it remains alone; but if it dies, it produces much grain.'* **John 12:24**

Relational conflicts

Every disappointing and distorted relationship will bring up emotive issues that have their roots in the past. When these roots are not addressed, they remain as *'roots of bitterness'* (**Hebrews 12:15**) and these go deep until we are even unaware of why a root is present.

But the shoot manifests itself in corrupt and sinful expression, surprising us sometimes that we have reacted in the way that we have. Therefore, we need God's help to deal with the root, so that the sinful shoot expressed can be addressed, changed and healed – perhaps with the wisdom of godly theotherapists.

Change is not something that we like – it makes us uncomfortable, as we pursue new ways of dealing with people, ourselves and our view of God. We have also been influenced by bad theology that states that, *'if anyone is in Christ, the new creation has come: The old has gone, the new is here!'* **2 Corinthians 5:17**.

Some have taken this to mean that their old sinful life is now dead, the past has gone, and they are new, different people who are no longer troubled by sin. Yet, experience tells us this is obviously a lie.

Misunderstanding of this verse will result in a type of schizophrenic Christianity, where we battle with the *'rising past, which forces itself into our present'*. This may present challenges as to whether we are really saved or not, or bring in doubts about our effectiveness as a Christian.

The *'new creation'* the scripture refers to, is that the old sinful life was dead in relationship to God and has now been made new by the regeneration of the Holy Spirit within us. Without this regeneration no one would choose to come to Christ due to our sin – **Ephesians 2:1-10, Colossians 2:13** – but once renewed we can have and enjoy a relationship with God. Sin still remains because we have a sinful nature, so there is still a battle that needs to be fought daily, until Christ returns for His Bride. **Romans 7**

Constantly, we are encouraged to put off that *'old sinful life and all its ways'* and put on the *'new righteous life'* in every area of our lives. This encouragement is not just within the spiritual realm, it affects the physical, the emotional, the social, our purpose and motivations, our work and career focus, affecting every sphere of our lives. This affects us not just when we attend church, but how we live outside the church too – in our everyday activities, our leisure, our work, our families, our time, our finances, our education, our relationships, etc. God sees all that we do, nothing escapes Him.

Dealing with relational conflicts

Subsequently, if we are all integrated relationally with each other to fulfil those desires (no one is an island – this is pathological, isolation is a defence mechanism that increases relational distress), then the relational angst needs to be addressed.

How is this possible? When we recognise an issue, do we go up to the individual concerned and tell them why the relationship is wrong? God forbid!

This is a method that has been advocated in the church, using scripture such as, *'you have heard that it was said to the people long ago, 'You shall not murder, and anyone who murders will be subject to judgment.' But I tell you that anyone who is angry with a brother or sister will be subject to judgment. Again, anyone who says to a brother or sister, 'Raca,' is answerable to the court. And anyone who says, 'You fool!' will be in danger of the fire of hell. Therefore, if you are offering your gift at the altar and there remember that your brother or sister has something against you, leave your gift there in front of the altar. First go and be reconciled to them; then come and offer your gift.'* **Matthew 5:2-24** (amp)

But where is this altar today – God has done away with it, when He divided the veil in two – **Matthew 27:51** (amp) – and *'has broken down the wall, the middle wall of hostility between us'* and God – **Ephesians 2:14** – so that we can now enter boldly into His presence. **Hebrews 4:16** (amp) The altar now is our heart before God.

This scripture, from **Matthew 5** above, has been used to address the conflict by going to the individual concerned and confronting them with the relational distress. This is possible, but sometimes this approach has been misapplied and used in such a way as to be more an act of revenge: *'I'm just going to tell you what it is that you have done or not done, said or not said, expected or not expected, demanded or not demanded, etc. – but I forgive you!'*

Often the unaware individual has no idea what the other is talking about! If so, it can exacerbate the grievance and possibly make it irreconcilable. All relational conflict is internal, and the method used above tries to absolve all responsibility for the way that the individual is dealing with their own internal relational conflict.

Internalisation is emotionally distressing, so, they project onto *'others'* and, displacing their feelings onto them, projecting their own angst. This amplifies the conflict greater than before, than if that individual had dealt with the conflict in the right way. First, the grieved individual must address the issue internally before God, then, if necessary, speak to the other person.

Right way to deal with conflict

What is the right way? It is a therapeutic process that will deal with the root, which will affect not just the initial presenting relationship, but other similar relationships too, that may have presented in the same way. It is a process that takes individuals over the *'Bridge of conflict resolution.'*

It is not a magical formula, or a prayer covering. It is dealing with the internal processes of our mind, to resolve the conflict. You need to look at how this relationship disturbs you – how does it make you feel, what does it make you think about, how reactive are you to this relationship and others like it?

Are you projecting externally what you are subconsciously feeling and thinking internally, which is manifesting an external response because the mind wants to resolve this internal conflict? This can be evidenced relationally by hostility towards others that may remind the individual of this conflict, or cause them to avoid particular relationships, or escape from dealing with any issues that cause internal distress? (This will be discussed in more depth later on).

Rejected people reject others

These questions and many more help to explore and enable the individual to face the reality of the internal conflict. All conflict is relational and conflict in relationships manifests as rejection and rejection is the essence of all sin.

Rejection is the opposite of acceptance and a failure to love the other. This is a consequence of sinful behaviours, thoughts, emotions, attitudes, etc. Rejection in relationships can make us emotionally, physically and spiritually immature, however, acceptance in relationships can heal us and make us whole.

The bible teaches us, *'if we freely admit that we have sinned and confess our sins, He is faithful and just and will FORGIVE us our sins and cleanse us from all unrighteousness.'* **1 John 1:9**

The unrighteousness is the expression of our sin and the cleansing is God's healing power to restore us and heal us from within.

Bridge of conflict resolution

Going over the *Bridge of Conflict Resolution* uses the four biblical tools of Theotherapy to heal relationships – when the relationship is healed, it heals a life. The four tools being:

Forgiveness,

Acceptance,

Surrender,

Theotherapeutic indifference (and substitution with love).

Tools of theotherapy

Forgiveness: God knows us intimately, so we need to confess everything to Him, before we even think about confronting the offending party. Confession is necessary for our benefit – not for God's. It is necessary because God needs us to see ourselves for who we really are. This is a principle laid down in **Genesis 3:9-13**.

God questions Adam and Eve in the garden, even though He already knew what they had done in disobeying the command. The questions were to cause Adam and Eve to see themselves. We need to see ourselves as God sees us and face the reality of our pain.

He is a relational God and delights in us sharing with Him – even though He knows us intimately about who we are. The confession part enables us to move towards forgiveness. We need to forgive the other that exposed the sin within us; this is an internal process, as we are dealing with our mind's response to it.

The Scripture states, *'forgive us our debts, as we also have forgiven our debtors'* –**Matthew 6:12, 14-15** – *'If you forgive people their trespasses your heavenly Father will also forgive you. But if you do not forgive others their trespasses, neither will your father, forgive you your trespasses.'*

So, forgiveness is a requirement, a command and has a purpose. Forgiveness is not dependent on a feeling to forgive – otherwise no one would forgive. It is based on making a decision to forgive the other. This decision changes the individual internally, which will heal the relationship – then it will be manifested externally, bringing healing and restoration.

This is true transformation and the result is healing that restores love between people – **1 Peter 1:22** – to *'love with a pure heart, without hypocrisy'* (in the Amplified version). This is the type of God's love, His Agape love towards us.

Forgiveness must be specific, so that it exposes the negative emotions that are damaging the mind, relationship and putting up barriers which are destroying the movement of love towards each other as we ought. A blanket spiritual statement of, *'I forgive you'*, does not allow the mind to resolve the internal angst within.

Negative emotions must be expressed to allow the healing of the mind. Negativity can be experienced in many ways: as fears, doubts, worries, insecurities, rejection, rebellion, anger, frustrations, pride, revenge, hatred, hostility, apathy, aggression, rage and a myriad of other negative emotions. Christ leads us by His example when He declared, *'Father, forgive them for they know not what they do.'* **Luke 23:34**

God has forgiven us and with that same forgiveness we can forgive others too. **Colossians 3:13**

Jesus' example shows us how to address issues when confronted by others. He always responded with love and compassion to everyone – even His accusers. What an example to learn from!

Acceptance: So, forgiveness opens the door to accepting the other. **Genesis 4:6-7**

Cain was angry with God and with his brother Abel. God challenged Cain and said, *'If you do well will you not be accepted? If you do not do well, sin lies at the door. And its desire is for you, but you should rule over it.'*

So, Cain could have accepted that Abel's sacrifice was accepted by God and his was not. In the acceptance of the event – of Abel and of God's purpose – Cain would not have fallen into sin. But as we know he did not accept the reality of God's choice and that caused his sin to grow to murder his brother.

So, acceptance of things that happen in life – whether they be from others, or of God's plan and purposes – keeps individuals in peace and stability. Acceptance of the way people are and of events that have happened in our lives means not trying to change them, or the expectation that they will ever change, or of trying to control them, or of the circumstances that brought the offence.

We stop resisting the offence caused because we cannot change the offence or the people in them. The past is the past, and what was, was. Acceptance frees individuals from the past. It is not our mandate to try and change others – God does the changing. **Psalm102:25-26**

Surrender: The acceptance of others allows the door of surrender to be opened and to let go of the perceived offence. **Jeremiah 38:17, Matthew 6: 20-21, 16:26**

Acceptance and surrender deal with not trying to work things out, or trying to impose your will onto others, and stop the desire to keep fighting against others, letting it go. Surrender says, *'I am making a decision to stop blaming and judging the individual concerned in the relational conflict and let it go.'* Surrender takes away the perceived feeling, or real feeling, that the other has power and control over us, because we surrender to God the situation and relationship involved.

Surrendering to God means I surrender to His will and purposes for my life and to everything that God brings into my life. The school of life is the teacher that draws us nearer to God. (Note, we do not surrender to the person, especially if that person is abusive).

But surrendering causes us to face up to the fear, thus making us vulnerable to that fear. This breaks the power and diminishes its power over us to control us. (But note again, this is not an external process – we acknowledge to face the fear internally, because we are dealing with the internal processes in the mind).

We face up to the individual concerned and give them permission internally, to say, or do, or think, or feel, whatever they choose to; so that we can deal with the reality and pain of the mental conflict. This process takes away the need to set up defence mechanisms, because we have faced it internally, and makes way to relate to others. If possible, after the therapeutic process it may provide a way to relate to the individual concerned externally, too.

Theotherapeutic indifference: As most of our issues are rooted deep in the past, we must recognise that we cannot change the past – these offences have happened, they cannot be changed. Therefore, we need to adopt another approach which states a *'so what'* attitude – because we have to move forward and on with our lives. So we make a decision to live in the present, by acknowledging the past as reality, but choosing to get past these offences – this is called *'theotherapeutic indifference.'*

This means I know the event took place but I'm not going to take on a *'victim mentality'* and let it determine and define how I live in the present. This theotherapeutic process is something that deals with the internal mental processes of the mind.

We have to take ownership and responsibility for what others may have done to us – before any thought of confronting or challenging others – so that we can deal with how it has affected us in the right way.

Dealing with the conflict that still needs God's healing

The pain and distress experienced needs to be substituted with a decision to choose to love the offending individuals. Choosing to love is what brings the healing. Now the external relationship conflict will be easier to deal with because the individual will have dealt with the internal emotional pain that was exposed in this relational issue.

Instead of reacting emotively the individual will be free to respond in a biblical, loving manner. Choosing to love means we give the love which God has given to us, to love and heal others – this is the same expression of God's love, when He forgives us our sins and loves us. It allows us to love sincerely and without hypocrisy. **1 Peter 1:22-2:3, 1 John 4:8-16, Romans 12:9-10, 2 Corinthians 1:4**

This therapeutic process – called *Theotherapy* – was coined by Rev. Dr. Mark Rivera's father, and continued by him as *Christian Counselling International* (CCI). This process is not always easy as the mind wants to protect itself from exposing the pain within. The mind does this by setting up all kinds of mechanisms, which need to be recognised and addressed so that the process is successful. Therefore, it is helpful to seek theotherapists who have been trained and accredited by CCI to assist the person in need.

Relational distress is seen in the Bride – the Church

The theotherapeutic process described before, is necessary if we are going to address the relational distress in the Bride. We have all witnessed the manifestation of relational break-down within the Bride that is being made ready for Christ's return.

How often we hear and read of the faithlessness of the church, of its leaders and worshippers in their relationship to God. Or the lack of application of God's truths towards each other; so that the world sees individuals who are denying God's word because they are not applying God's healing and salvation to themselves. The world sees this as hypocrisy – rightly so! It means that we have forgotten our purpose of being prepared for Christ's return.

This lack of application to make us more Christ-like is reinforcing the impotency of the Church – the church has become dysfunctional and ignored, so that its evangelism is falling on deaf ears. The world is not looking to the church for the help it needs. The church is failing Britain and it needs Christ to reconcile the hearts of men and women back to Him again. Change is needed and change must come.

The church is not perfect, we know – however, it is not excusable as a representation of the Body of Christ to remain as, *'unrepentant, sinful people.'* Perfection of the saints will never be fully achieved this side of heaven, but it must be the goal of the church – to make herself ready for the Groom, to pursue a life of holiness and righteousness that gives glory to God.

What is the right fear of God?

In the waiting period, we need to be reminded again that, *'The fear of the Lord, is the beginning of wisdom'* – **Proverbs 1:7** – but a feeling orientated theology has played down a Holy God, a God who is the Judge and will judge every sinful act that the church indulges in. We need to regain and teach again the *'right fear of the Lord.'*

Yes, God loves us and accepts us as we are, but He doesn't mean to let us live in any way that we choose and still claim to be called believers. Our unaddressed sins will mar our relationship with God, and maybe is the reason why He seems so distant to us. When we confess our sins, we regain that intimate, personal relationship with God again. **1 John 1:9**, **Psalm 51**

We do not need more external interventions; we need an internal heart search to be right with God. **Psalm 139: 23-24**

We pray for revival expecting God to send His Holy Spirit in power from on high, with dynamic interventions, but in every revival in the past the focus has been on confession that acknowledges the holiness of God – evidence from the 18th C. revival in Wales, the Awakenings in the US, a few examples. But the Holy Spirit is within us as believers – He can be grieved, if sin is present. **Ephesians 4:30-31**

Revivals change churchgoer's perspective, which re-orientates them back to their relationship with God, to the most important relationship – this often gets lost in the trappings and complexities of church life. This renewed perspective increases their fruitfulness and witness to the world.

Before we pray for revival, we have to let God search our souls; so that we are in a right relationship between GOD AND OURSELVES that is without hindrance, blot or wrinkle. Then the revival will come from within and be real, which will be manifested externally and will impact the people we meet. As we recognise God's Holiness, He will make the Bride ready to be presented to the Groom.

Divisions are inevitable as, *'the sheep are separated from the goats.'* **Matthew 25:31ff**

Many things have divided the church, both from within and without its walls, but we must renew our attention and focus again to the coming of our Lord Jesus Christ. Preparation can be uncomfortable and sometimes painful, but we need to encourage, actively engage in and declare that the Groom is coming for His Bride.

God is going to shake the church again, so we need to hear Him who is speaking to us and learn to be obedient to His voice. This may cause suffering, but we have Jesus' example

– he learned obedience to His Father through the things He suffered. **Hebrews 5:8, 12:25-29**

We need to be ready for a shaking of the church to be challenged and purified – the judgement of God will fall on the house of God first, so we will be perfected and ready for His return. **1 Peter 4:17**

What a wedding day that will be!

3 The bride becomes a wife

- Expectations
- Exclusivity
- Covenantal cost
- Covenantal promise
- Covenant keeper
- Marriage vows
- Personal covenant
- Covenantal breakdown – Hosea
- Abuses of the Bride
- Dying to self
- Godly leaders
- Independence is a sin
- Hope

The wedding day

In the same way as the church – the Bride – is going to be prepared for His coming, this is an analogy of the earthly relationship of the bride and groom preparing for marriage together.

The preparation and hard work that has gone before has led up to this pivotal moment. It's the day. The anticipation of this expected day has arrived. If the expectations of this day and all the preparations to make a perfect day were high and unrealistic, the day can turn out to be a disappointment. High expectations increase the stress involved with the preparations for this event.

Therefore, the bride needs to be reminded that the day is just the beginning of a life that will deepen that relationship; of the highs and lows that will inevitably accompany it. So, the bride needs to lower her expectations, reducing her stress and anxiety and stay in reality towards the future relationship. This applies to the groom, too – unrealistic expectations may create unnecessary tensions.

The bride and groom must also be aware that other people's expectations of them and of the wedding day, may also encroach on them, making demands on them and of the day which adds to the stress. Relatives' interventions need to be discussed in the preparation stage beforehand; as some relatives try to interfere in the relationship – setting up a precedent to be involved in the couple's marriage. Relatives' interventions can be the cause of marriage breakdown – these issues need to be addressed and recognised, so relatives do not contribute to marital conflicts.

However, our expectations of the Bridegroom and His return must remain high because God doesn't disappoint us. **Romans 5:5** He does what He says He will do. **Ezekiel 12:28** He will perfect His Bride. **Ephesians 5:26-27**

The Bride has been given to the Son as His reward – **John 17:6, 11-12** – and none shall be plucked out of His hand. So, we need to understand that the transformation within the church will be done by God as He promises to keep us.

Exclusivity

So many focus on the day and forget this day is a witness before the Lord (and I speak of the Christian marriage) and to others, that the bride and bridegroom have decided to give their commitment 100% to each other. This relationship is exclusive – Genesis states that the *'man shall leave his father and mother and be joined to his wife and they shall become one flesh.'* **Genesis 2:24**

This means that the marriage relationship is unique. Other people may feel they have a right to intervene – for example, Godfathers and Godmothers, or even spiritual mothers and fathers! – but this intervention must only be at the couple's request.

Some relatives will not let go of their children and let them grow up – this is a sad scenario and reflects on the parent's insecurities and on fulfilling their own needs through their children's marriage. Couples need to be aware of this issue and nip it in the bud, even if it may upset the relatives involved.

Covenantal Cost

Marriage starts off with a declaration of the covenant that is promised between the two individuals to each other who are joining together as one flesh. No more are there two separate individuals going their own way, pursuing their own desires, but together fulfilling each other's desires, to bring out the best in each other. Hebrew: עֵזֶר כְּנֶגְדּוֹ e*zer kenegdo* is the name, *'help-meet'* in English and means a wife suitable – who is oppositional to, who will bring out the best in the spouse, exploring their depth and potential.

Marriage should not be indulged in from a selfish perspective, it is a commitment to think of the spouse – this characteristic is a manifestation of love which begins and continues to grow and becomes the process of healing. The act of love is a process of giving and thinking of meeting the other's needs, but lust on the other hand is all about getting what I want, or taking from and having my own needs met.

From this perspective above, it is very helpful for the impending married couple to have gone through pre-marital counselling; as the couple are so *'in love'* they have blind spots to the other they think they should marry. A pre-marital counsellor will be able to expose these blind spots so that the couple have a realistic view of the commitment and the cost of the relationship.

Even with this intervention, their *'in-loveness'* may create a delusional belief, thinking that they will be able to overcome any difficulty that may arise, and many couples do overcome obstacles, but sadly many don't. To every committed relationship there is a cost. Jesus reminds us in **Luke 14:28** of the story of someone who wanted to build a tower, first they had to sit down and estimate the cost to see if they had enough money to complete it.

In an intimate relationship we do not know what the cost will be, but it must be considered so that there is an awareness of the price that might be paid. Some may feel the pre-marital counselling process is unnecessary, especially if the couple are more mature, and able to communicate their feelings adequately, allowing issues to be discussed openly within the relationship.

We are all self-absorbed and self-centred, pursuing those activities that would enhance what we want, when we want it, and that is usually now! This should change when that covenantal commitment is made, but what is it about this covenant that brings the healing mentioned earlier?

Covenantal promise

The covenant is a promise. To look at the covenantal principle we need to go further and understand the one who created covenants. God is the ultimate Covenant Keeper and, in the covenant He made with Noah – **Genesis 6:18** – God says, *'I will establish My Covenant with you and you shall come into the ark, you and your sons and your wife, and your sons' wives with you.'*

This covenant was made because the people on the earth at that time were people who had chosen to go their own way, *'The Lord saw that the wickedness of man was great in the earth and that every imagination and intention of all human thinking was only evil continuously.'* **Genesis 6:5**

As God watched the people turn away from Him to themselves, He regretted that He had made man and was grieved at heart. **Genesis 6:6** (amp)

The Omniscient God was not surprised, taken aback, nor phased by what was happening to the people. God in His benevolence had provided everything that humanity needed, yet they chose to reject Him. God's rejection of humanity due to sin, is expressed to us in language for us to understand; this is called anthropopathic language and is used so we can understand God's heart.

In our humanity, we understand what it feels like to give all to others who then decide to reject us. Despite God giving His people everything, we quickly and foolishly forget this and think we can become independent without God. **Psalm 14:1-2**

This is always to our detriment – **Isaiah 50:10-11**(amp) – and brings a curse on us.

Covenant keeper

So, the covenant made by God to Noah was that God would save them. Noah and his family were not chosen because they were sinless, but because they were favoured by God; therefore we continue to need a *'saving God'* and the power of salvation every day.

Without Him we lose direction, we become depraved and sinful, filled with anger and violence towards each other and corrupt, manifesting these things in all manner of perverseness. When we forget our need for a *'saving God,'* we become disconnected from our source and resource, which becomes destructive to our well-being.

God makes this covenant and we read, not only does He save them from the flood but also from the evil that caused God to respond – subsequently, He continues to be their Provider and Protector, He watches over Noah and his family and keeps them from harm. God makes a PROMISE and He is the ultimate Promise Keeper. Even when we are faithless, He is faithful for He cannot disown Himself. **2 Timothy 2:13**

Therefore, the marriage covenant is a vow – a promise made before God as a witness to Him. These vows should not be broken easily as God will call us to account for them. **Ecclesiastes 5:4-5, Deuteronomy 23:21-23**

Unfortunately, the change in law to *'no fault'* divorce has facilitated the easy breaking of the covenant relationship if it becomes difficult. But the Christian marriage covenant is based on the principles of God's keeping covenant towards us – God will never leave us or forsake us – **Hebrews 13:5** – even when life gets difficult.

Marriage vows

The most traditional version of the marriage vow is: *'I take you to be my wedded wife/husband. To have and to hold. From this day forward. For better or for worse. For richer or for poorer. In sickness and in health. To love and to cherish. Till death us do part. According to God's holy ordinance. And this is my solemn vow'.*

God chose us before the foundations of the world – **Ephesians1:4** – that we should be holy and blameless in His sight, even above reproach before Him in love. IN LOVE. God loves His people, He loves His church, His Bride, and chooses that we should be holy and blameless in His sight.

Now we know that the prospective bride and groom are not holy or blameless but we do know that, under the marriage covenant, they have separated themselves from others and made a decision to join themselves to each other forever. Like God – He has separated us from the world and chosen us to live with Him forever; all who belong to Him believe in Him and acknowledge Him as their Saviour, He forgives and redeems them to be right with Him. Forever, means to be with Him eternally when He returns for His Bride the church.

Personal covenant

God's Covenant is personal, is relational and is an intimate relationship – not physically as a husband and wife's relationship – but spiritually.

The intimacy of the marriage crosses every aspect of life, which the couple have to navigate to enhance each other's giftings. But they cannot save each other, for only God is the Saviour. The three-cord strand in **Ecclesiastes 4:9-12** encourages us to put God in the centre of the marital relationship – but only God can save us from our sins.

However, the two working together can help and nurture each other, to face up to and deal with their individual sins before God. Marital conflict is designed by God to reveal the self to the self, to expose the delusion we have concerning ourselves; so that God can heal the sin within.

When we experience an *'in love'* feeling with the other, we are often delusional and deceived about the characteristics of the other, as we overlook and justify the negative side of the individual – until we live with them and then the negative becomes surprisingly obvious as we become confronted by these things. This is why marriage, as said before, is for our continual healing.

Covenant breakdown

Marriage breakdown continues when the two individuals refer to their own resources to deal with the issues that are exposed. (Note. I am not speaking about abusive relationships). The covenant made on the wedding day says, despite what happens in our circumstances we will deal with it – *'for better or for worse, for richer or for poorer, in sickness and in health.'* That is COMMITMENT.

These are scenarios that we accept but don't truly think will happen to us because we are so *'in love'* that nothing will ever change that! We believe we have found the *'right person'*, so it will be love everlasting. However, the thought that this is the right person was RIGHT; God set you up with that *'right person'* – God in all His wisdom knows what you need to mature and heal you from within.

The overcomers are the ones who will grow in greater love, maturity and healing within themselves, with each other and with God. When there is conflict within the marriage – which is inevitable when two different people live together 24/7 – those that depend on God for His help and resources to overcome will win the crown of life. **James 1:12, Revelation 2:10**

Overcoming, even to the point of death, is to suffer in Christ's sufferings to attain to His glory. **Romans 8:17, Philllipians 3:10, 1 Peter 5:10**

Hosea is given as an example – God told Hosea to take Gomer, the daughter of Diblaim, as a wife and have children with her. Hosea knew full well that Gomer was a woman of harlotry, an unfaithful woman. Their three children came from this union: *'And the LORD said to him, "Name him Jezreel; for yet in a little while I will avenge the blood [that was shed in the Valley] of Jezreel and inflict the punishment for it on the house of Jehu, and I will put an end to the kingdom of the house of Israel. "On that day I will break the bow [of the military power] of Israel in the Valley of Jezreel." Then Gomer conceived again and gave birth to a daughter. And the LORD said to Hosea, "Name her Lo-Ruhamah (not shown mercy), for I will no longer have mercy on the house of Israel, that I would ever forgive them. "But I will have mercy on the house of Judah and will rescue them by the LORD their God, and will not rescue them by bow, sword, war, horses, or horsemen." Now when Gomer had weaned Lo-Ruhamah, she conceived and gave birth to a son. And the LORD said, "Name him Lo-Ammi (not my people), for you are not My people and I am not your God."* **Hosea 1:4-9** (amp)

God used the names of Gomer's children to show that He would reject Israel for the idolatry that they have sown – without love, without mercy and without pity – that He would no longer be Her Husband, *'for she is not my wife.'* **Hosea 2:2, 4**

Despite God's continual patience, grace, love and mercy towards His people, there comes a time when God says, *'enough'* and acts accordingly. What a devastating prospect, to experience this break up of a relationship with God our source and resource.

Gomer thought that she could turn to the world, to get the things that she desired, for many were ready to indulge her in the pursuit of her desires; not because they held her in high esteem or loved her with a true love, but because they knew they could feast on her weaknesses and use her for their own gain! Lust will always take advantage of those who want to indulge in it. **Hosea 2:5-13**

Abuse of the Bride

Today, some church attenders see the church, the Bride, in this way too. They go to church to get what they want and if they don't get it, they reject the church and God because they have a wrong perspective of what the church is for and of who God is. God is not our *'puppet on a string.'* God is not indulgent to our whims and desires. God will not support us in our sinful behaviours.

God is Lord over His church, His Bride, to perfect her for His Glory – however, God will reject His church, His people, His beloved, when, or to the extent that they plunge deeper into their idolatries. God is a God of Love and we emphasise this because it is an acceptable message to hear, but He is also the Holy God who judges – these are the messages we try to ignore, at our peril.

In His rejection of us, He still loves us and initiates circumstances to cause us to face ourselves and bring us back to our knees, in humility and repentance, so that His Bride will be perfected, honourable and acceptable to Him, the Bridegroom.

Thankfully, God keeps His Covenantal commitment to us and continues His Saving Redeeming Grace towards us. So we should be ever grateful He keeps us and sustains us because if it were dependent on us and our efforts, we have failed and will continue to fail. God is loving, merciful, faithful and continues to be the church's husband. **Hosea 2:16**

He promises to betroth himself to His Bride, to bring us to that place we need to be, ready for His return, **Hosea 2:19-23** (amp) He has promised He is coming – we need to be ready.

Dying to self

Even to the point of death – *'Till death do us part!'* Marriage is all about DYING – dying to self, selfishness, self-centredness, to my wants, my desires, my hopes, my dreams, my expectations. *'I say to you, unless a grain of wheat falls into the ground and dies, it remains alone; but if it dies, it produces much grain.'* **John 12:24-26**.

No one wants to die! Yet, the marriage ceremony states, *'till death us do part'*. We understand this as a reference to the one or the other spouse dying and leaving this earth. But before that final event, there is much dying that needs to be done daily in the marital relationship!

Divorces and separation happen consistently because neither of the individuals involved will repent, forgive and change their offending behaviours, because they always *'blame the other'* and will not take responsibility for their own actions in the relational breakdown. Some readers may find this a controversial statement, as we all want to exonerate ourselves from any guilt within the breakdown of the relationship. This is the very essence of sin.

Sin, full of pride says, *'I am right'*, *'I haven't done anything wrong'*, *'my response was justified and excusable'*, *'it's the other party that is at fault'* and such like corresponding statements can be made not to face up to the situation at hand. If *'love'* brought the two together, why can't *'love'* still sustain both individuals, to help and encourage each other despite their differences?

This *'covenantal relationship'* is not a switch that can be put on or off at a whim. What if we adopted this method to other areas of our lives, e.g. work, *'well, sometimes I will engage with work commitments and other times not,'* etc. – you wouldn't be employed for very long!

So, covenant promises are not to be based on feelings. I'm sure that Hosea was not basing his marriage on feelings, knowing his wife was going to be unfaithful to him. No, he based his marriage on the instruction of God to take this unfaithful wife.

This picture is a representation to us of the covenantal commitment of God and His Bride. It's not a pretty picture, but neither is the church we see today. All kinds of harlotries are being committed by the church as it syncretises itself with the world's philosophies and cultural sensitivities that are against God and His Word.

The church has lost its influence and power to advocate God's perspective in our lives. It has cowered into the background, encouraging *'leaders'* who will not challenge the status quo because of the consequences that they will face. Hosea states, *'My people are destroyed for lack of knowledge; because you the priestly nation have rejected knowledge, I will also reject you that you shall be not priest to Me; seeing you have forgotten the law of your God. I will also forget your children.'* **Hosea 4:6**

Some leaders in the church today are stumbling around in the dark because they have rejected the sound teaching of the Word of God; they preach, *'teaching that itching ears want to hear.'* **2 Timothy 2:3-4**

Those leaders who indulge in these lies will be rejected by God because they will be responsible for leading the people into error. **Hosea 5:1** (amp)

Godly leadership

Today, we need godly leaders who are willing to declare the Word of God, courageously and fearlessly, despite the accusations from the world, or even from within the church. Nothing has changed. The world has always *'hated'* the church and its teachings from the Word of God, so why are we reacting differently? **John 15:18-27**

We have lost our focus and mission in our presentation of the gospel of Jesus Christ. We have cowered into fear and compromised our allegiance to God's Word, by becoming the silent witness. Covid has exposed this expression of fear within us all with our surrender to it.

Fear is a terrible thing and some of us are more prone to fear than others. However, God knows that when we fear we are easily persuaded to take the easier option – that is, not to face our fears. Yet, there is a reason why the Word constantly tells us, *'Not to fear'* – for example, *'Fear not, for I am with you; be not dismayed, for I am thy God. I will strengthen you, yes, I will help you, I will uphold you with my righteous right hand.'* **Isaiah 41:10**

Are you still surrendering to fear in your life? If so, why? God has promised to be with us, He says, *'therefore go and make disciples of all the nations, baptising them in the name of the Father and of the Son and of the Holy Spirit, teaching them to observe all things that I have commanded you, and lo, I am with you always, even to the end of the age.'* **Matthew 28:19-20**

Jesus said, *'take up your cross daily and follow me'* – this means that every day we have to die to what we want and pursue actively what God wants, if we are His disciples. This is true of the marital relationship and in the Bride today. **Matthew 16:24-26**

And this is the tension – between what I want, versus what God wants of me. Will I lay down my life? Will I depend on my own source and resources to serve God? Or will I humble myself to acknowledge my dependence on God for everything that I do, I have, I own, I desire, etc.

Humility says, *'it's not about ME, it's about GOD AND HIS GLORY.'* Humility says, *'no'* to pride and independence without God. We have never been able to live this Christian life without our Saviour.

Those that choose to be independent without God are like those in Isaiah: *'Who is among you who reverently fears the LORD, who obeys the voice of His Servant, yet who walks in darkness and deep trouble and has no shining splendour in his heart? Let him rely on, trust in, and be confident in the name of the LORD and let him lean upon and be supported by His God. Behold all you enemies of your own selves, who attempt to kindle your own fires and work out your own plans of salvation, who surround and gird yourselves with momentary sparks, darts and firebrands that you set aflame! Walk by the light of your self-made fire and of the sparks that you have kindled for yourself, if you will! But this shall you have from My hand; you shall lie down in grief and in torment.'* **Isaiah 50:10-11** (amp)

Independence is a sin

INDEPENDENCE is a product of the fall and is sin! Before sin entered the world Adam and Eve were totally dependent on God for all their needs. When they became independent from God they had to rely on their own resources.

Independence breaks up relationships, as seen in divorces, separations, churches in cliques or church splits – and even in nations – as individuals forget that only in Christ alone are we saved. Independence says, *'I don't need help,' 'I can do this on my own,' 'I don't need people,' 'I am right, it's others who are wrong.'*

Humility says, *'I am a sinner, who is saved by Christ alone and need God's continual help. His help enables me to sustain others, to guide and lead, to help, to heal, to deliver, to protect, to provide, to give assurances and encouragement, to love and to give mercy. His help gives me all I need for myself and to be there for others.'*

All I have is in Christ and He is all I need. **Galatians 2:20**

This verse does not justify the *'Jesus and me only'* complex some Christians have fallen into, but it expounds our reliance and dependence on God for everything we need – this includes building relationships.

The opposite of independence is an unhealthy dependence on the church, that has an expectation that the church should meet all of the individual's needs – this is not the purpose of the church. Some have substituted the church for their *'family,'* because they are trying to escape and not face up to the pain of their own dysfunctional family. This substitution places an unhealthy dependence and burden on the church that will not be able to fulfil the demands placed on it.

This escape mechanism uses the church as a safe place, but this is delusional because the church is made up of people, who are sinners saved by grace – trying to make the church and church people safe keeps individuals cocooned within the safety of its walls. This means that the Great Commission to go out and share the gospel is curtailed.

There is sometimes an expectation that people should be invited to come within the safety of the walls of the church. Or conversely, that outside the church is not a safe place, fraught with all kinds of dangers and evils to ensnare the unsuspecting saint. This substitution towards the church as a safe place diminishes its purpose and is IDOLATRY. It is not depending on God to sustain and keep us to be the people and to be the church that God has called us to be.

Therefore, God wants us to have a healthy interdependence on each other and a total dependence on Him for everything that we need. Interdependence is the balance between the two extremes of independence and dependency. This can only be achieved when God is in the centre of all our relationships. So, as the married couple need to put God in the centre, so does every relationship we hold both within and outside the church.

Hope

God's covenantal promise always brings hope and hope never disappoints us. **Romans 8:5** Despite the demise of the church, the Bride and its leadership, these are being kept today.

In the Valley of Achor, in the times of trouble, there is the door of hope and expectation. **Hosea 2:15** The Bride will again refer to God as, *Ishi* – my husband. **v.16** The two shall be reconciled to each other again, as the Bride addresses the idolatry she has fallen into.

This reconciliation is also available to those who are experiencing marital conflicts; when both parties address the sin within and deal with the influences on the relational issues – then the marriage can be restored. God never gives up on us, neither should we give up on each other when there is conflict. God's covenantal example is the same example we make on the wedding day – of commitment, faithfulness and fidelity. If we cannot do this in the most intimate of relationships, how will we be able to express it to others outside of this relationship?

First, we must be right with God, then we can address relational conflict within the marriage and towards other relationships too.

This applies to individuals who are single too. As we relate to God dealing with our sins, we will be freer to relate to others, as the Bride is the representation of the Body of Christ. The result is that relationships within the church will become more harmonious, expressing a unity within our diversities, to fully express God on this earth.

This does not mean we all have to be the same – it's not about *'conformity,'* having to all agree on the same things – but individually and together, we can manifest distinct gifts for the maturing of the Bride. **Ephesians 4:11-16**

4 – Maturation

- **God's Sovereignty**

- **His Way**

- **Bad theology**

- **Trust**

- **Vulnerability**

- **Idolatry**

- **God first**

Maturation is the process of growing up into mature individuals. Relational conflicts can hinder this process of maturing and the therapeutic process discussed enables individuals to deal with those issues, and be transformed to become more like Christ. These have been highlighted so that lessons can be learned and used within the church, so that the Bride of Christ would be presented mature.

Maturation says, *'I'm growing up', 'I am learning to deal with conflicts in a mature way.'* No one likes to see adults who are immature in their responses to others. This is a sad present-ation, as it projects an abuse of the potential that could be released if the immaturity were not present.

God's Sovereignty

Maturation says, *'it's not about me, it's about God!'* Despite this, many Christians today try to play down, or even reject that it is God who is in control and is Sovereign over all. To accept this belief is to surrender ourselves over to God's rule.

This is not a popular concept that is acceptable to us in the 21st C. – the idea of being controlled by anyone is abhorrent and reprehensible – we believe that we are free beings, able to make our own choices, make our own plans, etc.

Yet, scripture tells us, that man's mind plans his ways but the Lord directs his steps. **Proverbs 16:9** Also, *'For I know the plans I have for you, says the Lord, thoughts and plans for welfare and peace and not for evil, to give you hope in your final outcomes.'* **Jeremiah 29:11** (often taken out of context, to mean that life is going to be rosy!)

His Way

Yet, our plans do not always align with God's plans – for example, in the life of Joseph, we know that God's plan for him was to save Israel – however, the way He got Joseph to that point was not a plan Joseph would have imagined for himself.

Joseph was betrayed by his brothers, kidnapped and sold to slavers, was accused of rape by Potiphar's wife, was forgotten in jail despite giving the interpretation of the butler's and baker's dreams. Then the butler remembered Joseph when Pharaoh had a dream that no one could interpret, so Joseph was called into the palace. All these events in Joseph's life bought him nearer to the fulfilment of God's purpose for him.

In the same way, the trials that we encounter are not the ones that we would choose, or have expected, and can therefore evoke a distorted and misinterpreted view of a loving God! Many who have suffered in life – all do! – may project their sufferings onto God and conclude that they are under some kind of curse, because they feel they have mistaken God's purposes.

This may result in them blaming God for their understanding of His purposes for them and questioning His love towards them. Despite this, the sufferings, disappointments, misunderstandings of God and His purposes, ARE all a part of God's plans for us and bring us closer in our understanding of who God really is.

Bad theology

Bad theology will produce bad psychology and screwed up immature people. So, the outcome of rejecting the Sovereignty of God, encourages a sense of independence, entitlement and pride. Total reliance on God doesn't question the revelation of His plan in our lives.

It just says, *'Yes, Lord,'* wherever you want to take me, whatever circumstances you give me, *'I will rejoice in the Lord'* – just like **Habbakkuk 3:17-19** (amp): *'though life is not panning out as I thought it might, I will surrender my understanding, my thoughts, my working out of my plan, my career, my church, my ministry etc., I will surrender it all and accept that this is the plan of God for my life and everything that that involves.'*

We see this in the example of Ruth when she replied, *'Don't urge me to leave you or to turn back from following you; for where you go, I will go, and where you lodge, I will lodge. Your people shall be my people and your God my God. Where you die, I will die, and there I will be buried. May the LORD do so to me, and more also, if anything but death parts me from you.'* **Ruth 1:16-17** (amp)

This is the way of acceptance and surrender to God that brings peace and security, hope and love, in the confidence and knowledge that God knows what He is doing and will bring good out of it all. *'All things work together for good for those who love God who are called according to His purposes.'* **Romans 8:28**

Trust

This kind of acceptance and surrender leads us to trusting in God, despite what we see in our circumstances. Lack of trust is the consequence of bad relationships, of being let down, of being disappointed or betrayed by others; and the more significant the relationship the greater degree of brokenness that manifests.

Trust in others, once lost, is difficult to recover from and projects itself onto future relationships. Consequently, we need to recognise our understanding of trust and what it means. Why do we make so many errors when it comes to trusting others? It's probably not the first time that you have experienced your trust in people to fail. We have trusted the wrong people, or others have trusted us and we have not met their expectations of us.

Relationships take time and sometimes we rush in far too easily and share our souls, to discover that the individuals we have related to have shared your soul with everyone else. Gossip hurts, gossip devastates and gossip ruins relationships!

This manifests itself in the church, *'If you bite and devour each other, watch out or you will be destroyed by each other.'* **Galatians 5:15**

In the same way, criticism of each other within the marital relationship and comparisons with other marital relationships, is a recipe for disaster. This sets up feelings that, *'the grass is always greener on the other side,'* that creates a feeling of deficit that the individual is missing out on something better. This is when the heart starts to wander away from the commitment of the relationship.

Vulnerability

But even if we have taken the time and exercised prudence, our relationships can still backfire. The longer the relationship continues and deepens, the greater the opportunity for trust to be broken. To trust means to make yourself vulnerable to another and this can be abused, giving more fuel for the fire the more you think you know about the other individual.

David experienced this, in **Psalm 55:12-14**, when he describes that even his closest friends had betrayed him – not just anyone, but someone he used to have close fellowship with.

So, let's be honest, it *will* happen, trust *will* be broken – therefore, our trust must not be in people, but in the God who is Sovereign over the people. We trust God first, and trust Him with the people He places in our lives. This may not stop the betrayal, disappointments and failures in relationships, but at least we can be sure that whatever relationship has broken down, God knows about it and has set it up, to draw us into a closer relationship with Him. **Hosea 6:1**

Idolatry

'Do not be confused, we are all sinners in need of a Saviour, if we set others up on pedestals in our hearts, we are setting up idols which take the place of God'.

Anything can be set up as an idol, and this includes church leaders, theologians, organisations, people, etc. These idols will fail or our view of them will diminish because God will cause them to fail. God has said, *'You shall have no other idols before me or worship them.'* **Exodus 20:3ff**

Our God is a jealous God and has taken ownership over those who belong to Him, *'I am my beloved and He is mine.'* **Song of Solomon 6:3**

His commitment is forever towards us. How many leaders have fallen because they have allowed their followers to idolise them and have stood in the place where God should have been? This becomes a hindrance to the development and maturation of an individual's relationship with God.

God first

God said, *'You are my people! And they shall say, you are my God!'* **Hosea 2:23**

'I will be their God and they shall be my people.' **Ezekiel 37:27, 2 Corinthians 6:16**

God first.

So, we need to repent of trusting others before God. God will never let us down, but people will, *'And if it is evil in your eyes to serve the LORD, choose this day whom you will serve, whether the gods your fathers served in the region beyond the river, or the gods of the Amorites in whose land you dwell. But as for me and my house, we will serve the LORD.'* **Joshua 24:15**

When our trust has been broken, we need to deal with all the emotional responses that accompany that – to go over the *Bridge of Conflict Resolution*, as described in chapter one, or find a theotherapist who will help you follow this biblical therapeutic resolution – otherwise, the rejection that gets set in with broken trust will become a *'root of bitterness,'* as mentioned earlier, and impact future relationships.

5 The Image of God

- **Complementarianism**

- **Authority**

- **Domination**

- **Fruit bearers**

- **Spiritualisation**

- **Fruit in marriage**

- **Witness to the world**

- **Love self**

- **Dead fruit**

The character of the Bride is one that represents the image of God and of His love. **Ephesians 5:32** Men and women were created in the *'image and likeness of God.'* **Genesis 1:27** The image is a reflection of the glory and character of God.

So, together both men and women reflect the attributes of God, to complement (the thing that completes, or brings to perfection) each other and to reveal the completeness of who God is. Both are needed to fulfil this mandate and to emphasise one sex over the other would be to negate the fulfilment of the command to, *'be fruitful, multiply, fill the earth and subdue it, and to have authority over the fish of the sea, over the birds of the air, and over every living thing that moves on the earth.'* **Genesis 1:28** (This is referencing the marriage scenario, however, this does not suggest that single people cannot express the completeness of God, but this is not the topic of this book).

Complementarianism

– men and women are different and have different functions

Some might object to this because the Fall in **Genesis 3** has corrupted the purposes of God for men and women to reveal God to the world. Men and women are different! It's obvious – each sex, male or female, bring different perspectives to the relationship and each sex should be respected and honoured for their different perspectives.

The sex divide exposes many issues, e.g. chauvinism or feminism, that can be expressed within the Bride. These divisions can become extreme and polemical exposing the insecurities of each, namely the issues of *'authority,' 'power'* and *'control,'* etc.

It is stated that the husband is the Head of the wife as Christ is the Head of the church. 1 **Corinthians 11:3** But *'I want you to know that the head of every man is Christ, the head of woman is man, and the head of Christ is God,'* and in **Ephesians 5:23**, *'for the husband is head of the wife, as also Christ is head of the church; and He is the Saviour of the body.'*

Authority issues

These verses can raise strong objections from both sexes, if parental upbringing has abused and distorted the use of authority, power and control. Unfortunately, if this has occurred – and we all have sinful parents whose parenting has been imperfect – we can subconsciously project this onto God and onto the spouse.

Sometimes this may result in resisting God's ultimate control over our lives, which will hinder the intimacy of our relationship with Him. This may be expressed in either the man or woman, as a self-protective, dominating, reaction in response to the above.

If this is evidenced then it is advisable for those individuals to engage in therapy to help them address those issues, because it will affect any similar authoritarian relationship. Christ does not dominate His body, He loves her and takes care of her. **Ephesians 5: 28-29**

So, the attitude of love must be the ultimate goal here. If you have to force your views on another, you are WRONG and out of sync with God – your attitude to your fellow believer is wrong and your presentation is not one of love, but the opposite.

Domination

An overbearing, dominating husband is unbiblical, and manifests a lack of love and an insecurity in himself. When this is projected towards the wife, it is witnessed in very insecure, fearful and worried wives – a sad consequence. On the other hand, neither is it right that the wife becomes subservient, to allow the husband to treat her like a doormat, as both these responses open the door to domestic abuse.

However, neither is it right to see a wife who feels she has to lead in the home, because the husband is abdicating his responsibilities. The wife who overcompensates for the husband in this scenario, ends up emasculating the husband's position and role in the home. This creates resentments, and tensions abound when these approaches are out of sync with God's word. They do not reflect the biblical admonition of Christ loving the Church, and consequently do not bring the fruitfulness that God commanded of Adam and Eve, in **Genesis 1:28**. The fruitfulness described in Genesis is not just about procreation, but it extends to every area of our lives. **Psalm 1:3** and **Galatians 5:22-23**

Fruit bearers

Bearing fruit is hard work – first you need to recognise why the fruit is not developing as you would expect, this means being honest with yourself. Second, you need to find the root of the problem, as mentioned before, because the shoots will manifest the sustainability and effectiveness of the root.

Thirdly, you need to deal with the relationship at the point in time where the conflict occurred that produced the defective root in the life of the individual. There is a saying that, *'time is a healer'* – this is not true, it just distances the individual from the pain that had occurred. You cannot go back to the time the offence occurred physically, but it can be dealt with internally in the mind. It is at all these points 1-3 that many believers go awry.

Spiritualisation

This intervention of spiritualisation dissociates individuals from their experiences that they have encountered, distancing them and removing them from the pain. Instead of facing up to the pain – and we do experience pain and suffering in life – we displace it onto God and spiritualise our relational conflicts. This delays the healing process as the mind starts to fragment to try and deal with the internal conflict.

This separation leads to compartmentalised Christianity – separating out the spiritual from the secular psychological distress. However, the fruitfulness that God commands in **Genesis 1**, is to encompass every aspect of our lives – the spiritual, the psychological and the physical. God is the ultimate pruner and will cut off every dead branch that doesn't bear fruit – **John 15** – so fruitfulness means addressing all these issues.

This *pneuma-psycho-somatic* (spirit, soul and body) approach found in Theotherapy, addresses the integration of the self to prevent the fragmentation and compartmentalisation – which, if it occurs, can then delay and even prevent, God's healing process from taking place.

Fruitfulness in marriage

Within the marital relationship between a man and a woman, this fruitfulness can be achieved, as each give to the other what is lacking – exposing and challenging what needs to be changed. The orientation of this fruitfulness is to return to the state before sin entered the world, where everything was uncontaminated and undefiled by sin's presence.

Obviously, this is not possible until Christ returns for His Bride and we cannot return to the Garden of Eden. But we can return internally to that state of total dependence on God where God provides for us and meets our every need. Dependence on God means that we will know God's presence when we encounter the storms of life – His love for us will enable us to remain stable and secure whatever it is that we face.

'And the peace of God, which surpasses all understanding, will guard your hearts and your minds in Christ Jesus.' **Phillipians 4:7**

This is the outcome of dealing with the emotional angst of relational conflicts. *'He will keep him in perfect peace whose mind is stayed on Him.'* **Isaiah 26:3**

Together, as we practice working out fruitfulness within our marriages, this experience and principle can then be transferred to other relationships within the Bride of Christ.

Loving witness to the world

How many churches have become ineffective in their witness because their relationships are unloving? **Galatians 5:14-15**

'And this is how they will know that you are my disciples if you have love one for the other.' **John 13:35**

Maybe the criticism of the church as being hypocritical is justified! Why is our witness ineffective? Perhaps it's because we are looking to others to supply that lack of love within ourselves and then projecting it onto people in the church to meet that need. But they cannot and must not fill this lack, because this then becomes idolatry. All substitutionary relation-ships to replace God are a form of idolatry.

This love must come from the significant figures that could have shown us that love, but weren't able to, for whatever reasons. When this love is absent, confused, deficient, it is reflected in a low self-esteem, low self-worth and all kinds of negative reactions – resulting in a consequential lack of love towards the self. But if there is little or no self-love, how can we fully love our neighbours as ourselves, both within and without the Bride of Christ?

Love self

Jesus answers the question, *'Who is my neighbour?'* with, *'You shall love your neighbour as yourself. There is no other commandment greater than these.'* **Mark 12:31**

How can you love yourself when the love portrayed to you as a child has been imperfect? These psychological issues run deep and set up a cycle of rejection. Yet, Christ has taught us to, *'honour our father and mother.'* **Exodus 20:12**

This is difficult and must not be minimised, or spiritualised, because we are now believers. It must be dealt with therapeutically, so that it doesn't cause further damage within the Bride of Christ.

If the hurt from significant figures has not been dealt with therapeutically, it can manifest in the family home and in the marital relationship. So, it is absolutely essential that the hurt and pain is not glossed over, suppressed or depressed – the consequences of the lack of love must be healed.

Those who are married may be surprised when speaking that they sound or behave in ways like their mother or father, or both, or may see their parents in the spouse they have married. This can be a shock, especially if there is still emotional angst in the parental relationship that has not been addressed – this can be true even if the parents have died.

If the individuals have not experienced that healing, it may impact on the marriage and even on relationships within the

Bride, too. So, if this speaks to your heart, seek out a theo-therapist to deal with this conflict and find healing. Sometimes believers speak of *'spiritual mothers and fathers'* which is good, if the above has been dealt with. However, if they are being used as a substitute, this is unhelpful and places demands and expectations on the *'spiritual mothers and fathers'* that God did not intend – in fact, it is idol worship!

Dead fruit

Bad fruit smells and contaminates other fruit close by, *'bad fruit destroys itself'* – it will eventually become infertile, not able to reproduce. So, fruitlessness expresses a withholding of the glory of God from being revealed on the earth. God's command is to be fruitful and bear much fruit – this is not just a reference to procreation, but to every aspect of our lives.

Good fruit can be enjoyed by everyone and God's intention is that this good fruit can be shared for all to enjoy. It encourages and builds others up, so that the witness of the Bride can be a reflection to the world of the creative and life-giving healing that Christ alone can bring. The complete manifestation of His healing power will be manifested on His return.

6 Consummation

- **Sex is a gift**

- **Gender Fluidity**

- **The influence of society**

- **Chosen by God**

- **Heroes of the faith**

- **Eternal Vision**

- **Bridegroom returns**

Intimacy

The married couple are now free to enjoy the intimacy and legality of their new covenant relationship. This new exclusive relationship can be both a positive and negative experience. Each individual will have had relationships that will have equipped the individual, or not, for the expressing of intimacy. The relationship must be one of openness and honesty based on, *'speaking the truth in love.'* **Ephesians 4:15**

This may be new territory for many and difficulties in intimate expression may result in secrecy, withholding information, not sharing self with the other correctly, prudishness – that is being ashamed of the exposure of nakedness, separateness of not engaging with the other, distancing and lack of emotional expression, care or concern for the other, etc. These issues must be addressed, so that the fullness of intimacy, freedom within the marriage and enjoyment in the relationship can be grounded on a firm foundation.

Sex is God's gift

Sex is a good gift that was given and created by God; however, corrupt minds have polluted the beauty and purity of sex and many have been influenced through the media, social media, and internet sites, that have enticed individuals to pursue pornography, which is contaminating men and women's minds, distorting this precious gift.

Pornography is a growing concern and 68% of church-going men and over 50% of pastors view porn on a regular basis. Of young Christian adults 18-24 years old, 76% actively search for porn. Not just adults, but children, are being exposed to unnatural sexual images and this is found in education in the gender identity ideology, as well as in many social media domains. Eleven is the average age that a child is first exposed to porn, and 94% of children will see porn by the age of 14! **Barna Group/ Covenant Eyes** (2020).

The recent release of the film, *Sounds of Freedom,* based on a true story, has highlighted and exposed the end consequences of pornography. Monteverde, A.G., Director, (2023).

Gender fluidity

The promotion of gender fluidity has created confusion in young children about their identity. This assault on sex and gender issues is laying ground for more individuals to grow up with a perverted and distorted view of sex and gender expression.

Referrals to the *Tavistock Clinic* in the UK have escalated astronomically. There was a significant increase of referrals from 2009-19 – went from 77 referrals to 2,590, with the highest increase in the 15-year age group, with 1,740 girls to 624 boys in 2019.

This study showed that of the teenagers between the age of 12-15 who had started on puberty blockers, 98% also went on to treatment with cross-sex hormones – this is the next stage to gender reassignment. Today, children as young as three years old are being referred to gender identity clinics! The study also showed that there was no evidence of psychological improvement.

The influence of society

The church has not escaped this societal confusion, which has led to some believers becoming influenced by this lowering of standards that God has laid down for the purity of sex. Thus, it needs to be exposed and addressed within the church as many need to be reminded of what the Word of God does say.

The beauty and purity of sex needs to be reclaimed, so that married individuals are not hindered in being sexually intimate with their spouse. Any previous influences can create obstacles in the relationship, so need to be dealt with, so it doesn't affect the marriage. Consequently, God wants to heal men and women emotionally, as well as spiritually and physically, so we can become fully mature. *Covenant Eyes* is a useful resource to help individuals. Also, a useful resource here is Tim Chester's book, *Captured by a Better Vision: Living Porn Free*.

The marriage

This is the day when the Bride is joined to the Groom. Christ will come to take us home to be with Him, to the place that He has already prepared for us. **John 14:2**

The consummation day says, *'my beloved is mine and I am His'* – **Song of Solomon 2:16, 6:3,7:10** – and Christ's desire is for her, the church – she is His Bride and nothing can change that.

Many have tried to destroy the church, but she continues waiting for His return – *'nothing will separate us from the love of God'* – **Romans 8:35ff** – and *'the gates of Hell shall not prevail against her.'* **Matthew 16:18** This relationship between the Bride and the Groom is for eternity.

Chosen by God

The Bride has been chosen by Christ, in the same way that the marital couple have chosen each other. It is a relationship that is founded and built on love, and this *'love never fails.'* **1 Corinthians 13**

On the Bridegroom's return, we will be able to enjoy the freedom of our love towards Christ, unhindered by sin. We can only imagine what this is like as our corrupt imaginations have been tainted by sin, so we will only scrape the surface of what this ultimate union will be like. But we can revel in this anticipation – however misrepresented by our minds – of an expectation and hope that we must hold in our thoughts as we engage with the *'here and now'*. This *'hope does not disappoint us.'* **Romans 5:5**

This is the glory which we are waiting for – our eternal salvation.

Heroes of faith

The heroes of the faith, while waiting for their promise to be fulfilled, held on in faith, not to the fulfilment of the promise but onto the GIVER of the promise. They held on beyond the promised expectation, because they were looking for something greater than the promise, which is their eternal home. **Philippians 3:20**

'These all died in faith, not having received the promises, but having seen them afar off were assured of them, embraced them and confessed that they were strangers and pilgrims on the earth.' **Hebrews 11:13**

'They did not receive the promise.' **Hebrews 11:39**

'Their desire was for something better and that is a heavenly city. Therefore God is not ashamed to be called their God, for He has prepared a city for them.' **Hebrews 11:16**

Eternal vision

Consequently, we are reminded to fix our eyes on what is eternal and not temporal. **2 Corinthians 4:18**

Because in a moment everything can change – like Enoch. **Genesis 5:24**

The Bride will be transported into God's glory having been prepared and made ready for the Bridegroom. The perishable body tainted by sin will become imperishable, and the mortal become immortal and free from death. Then we shall see all that was promised that, *'death is swallowed up in victory.'* **1 Corinthians 15:51ff**

Let us be continually reminded that God has promised us a world without sin, just as in the beginning of Genesis. We will experience the totality of harmony of love towards God, towards others and within ourselves – in total peace, pure love, perfect acceptance, real healing, completely prosperous in everything we need, one in heart with the Father, His Son and Holy Spirit. A total integration of the personality is to be in all our relationships, so that God who created us for His purposes will receive the glory due to His Name.

What an amazing day this will be! To be united with the Triune God, one with Him, as Christ is with His Father. **John 17:21ff**

And Christ asks the Father, *'I desire that they also whom you have entrusted to me (as your gift to me) may be with me where I am, so that they may see My glory, which you have given me (your love gift to me) for you loved me before the foundation of the world.'* **John 17:24** (amp)

The Bridegroom returns

This is the HOPE that we have, because Christ has not forgotten His church and is waiting for the Word from the Father, to come and claim His Bride. As we get entangled in the day's affairs, let us encourage each other and talk often of His return and how we can be ready. **Malachi 3:16-17**

HE IS COMING. **Malachi 4:1** So, it matters how we respond, as we wait daily for Him. *'The Sun of Righteousness will arise with healing in His wings and His beams and you shall go forth and gambol like calves released from the stall and leap for joy.'* **Malachi 4:2** (amp)

There will be healing and joy on that day, now *'all things will be made new'* – **Revelation 21:4-5** – no more death, pain, tears, grief-sadness, darkness, evil, sorrow, anxiety, depression, fear, etc.

This day has been confirmed by the angel, God's messenger to John, and written down for us in **Revelation 22:16-17** (amp): *'I am the Root, the Source and the offspring of David, the radiant and brilliant morning Star. The Holy Spirit and the Bride, the church, those whose names are written in the Lamb's book of life, the true Christians, say, 'Come!''*

Yes, come, Lord Jesus!

About the author:

Heather Owen is a retired nurse, RGN, and has a BSc (Hons) in *Psychology* and MSc in *Abnormal and Clinical Psychology* from Swansea University. She has been married for thirty-nine years to Rev. Chris Owen and has three grown up young men, each pursuing their own walk with God.

Since 1990 she started training in Theotherapy and recently completed a *Doctorate in Theotherapy* (DTT) – awarded by *Christian Counselling International*, based in Puerto Rico. The principles of Theotherapy have enabled the pursuit of the above educational achievements and brought healing, to build solid relationships with others.

Currently she teaches and counsels in the modality of Theotherapy, online and in person. This has allowed many people to find the healing that they need, and to go on and pursue their own callings in ministry. She says, *'It is a joy to see how Theotherapy works in and heals individuals lives.'*

This book was a long time coming, was inspired by God and hopefully is the first in the *Joy Series*.

Acknowledgements

I would like to give thanks to all those who took the time to read, edit and comment on the draft copy of this book. Thank you for your patience.

I would also like to thank Rev. Dr. Mark Rivera for taking the time to write the prologue and for encouraging me to explore my potential.

Also, to the publisher in giving me the opportunity to make this book available.

I would also like to thank members of my family – to Chris, David, Tom and Josh – for their constant support and encouragement not to give up and pursue this endeavour. (Hoping they all buy many copies!).

And lastly to God for His inspiration and help in writing on this topic.

Bibliography

All scripture references are from the **New King James Version**, unless otherwise stated.

Amplified Bible, (1987). Zondervan Publishing House, Grand Rapids, Michigan, USA.

Barna group and Covenant Eyes. (2020). Kingdom Works Studios https://conquerseries.com/15-mind-blowing-statistics-about-pornography-and-the-church/

Census, 2021. www.ons.gov.uk/peoplepopulationandcommunity Accessed 01/23.

Chester, Tim. (2010). *Captured by a better vision: Living porn free*. Inter Varsity Press.

Cohabitation agreement. www.lawdepot.co.uk/contracts/cohabitation-agreement Accessed 01/23

Easy divorce. www.gov.uk/divorce Assessed 01/23.

Kabic, Jelena (2022). **Divorce Rate UK** (21+ Mind-Boggling Facts & Stats). review42.com/uk/resources/divorce-rate-uk Accessed 01/23.

Manning, W., Smock, P.J. (2009). *Divorce-proofing marriage*. Young adults' views on the connection between cohabitation and marital longevity. *National Council on Family Relations*.

Moreno, L. **European values source**. (2008). *Marriage as an outdated institution* 1990-2008.

Monteverde, A.G., Director, (2023). *Sound of Freedom* film.

New King James Version. (1982). www.eden.co.uk/king-james-bibles

RELATE www.relate.org.uk Accessed 01/23.

Rivera, Mario Rev., Rivera, Mark Rev. Dr. (1959). **Christian Counselling International**, Santa Barbarossa Presbyterian Church, Puerto Rico. *www.christiancounsellinginternational.org*

Socrates/Plato (5/6th B.C.). **In the Republic**, 375 B.C.

Tavistock's Gender Identity Development Service (GIDS) (2011). Tavistock and Portman Health Trust. https://www.bbc.co.uk/news/uk-55282113 Accessed 01/23.

The Marriage Covenant www.churchofengland.org/prayer-and-worship/ worship-texts-and-resources/common-worship/marriage

Wright, N. (1992). **The Pre-marital counselling handbook**. Moody Publishers. ISBN 10 0802463827. ISBN 13 : 978-0802463821

UK Parliament. Documents. **Common law marriage and cohabitation** https:// commonslibrary.parliament.uk/research-briefings/ sn03372/

Other books from **Precious Oil Publications**:

Fiction & non-fiction by **Raymond McCullough:**

Six Hours fiction series, (based on bible prophecy):

The *Arrows* bible prophecy series
(hitting one prophetic target at a time):

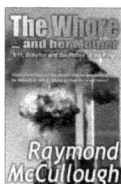
Bible prophecy identifying end-time Babylon

Testimonies from around Ireland

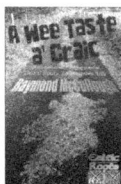
Scripts from *Celtic Roots Radio* show

Fiction by *Gerry McCullough:*

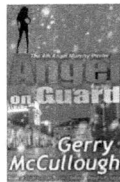

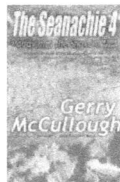

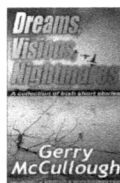

available from *Amazon* worldwide

www.ingramcontent.com/pod-product-compliance
Lightning Source LLC
Chambersburg PA
CBHW071927020426
42331CB00010B/2757